THE GREAT SCIENTISTS

Galileo Galilei

Kavita Sharma and Aaliya Roy Kundal

Om KIDZ
An imprint of Om Books International

Do you ever look up at the stars and wish they looked bigger? Have you ever seen the planet Mars as a tiny dot and wondered what colour it might be? A scientist called Galileo Galilei made it possible for you to do that! He created powerful telescopes to see stars and planets far away in the galaxy!

Galileo Galilei, popularly called just Galileo, was born on 15 February 1564 in the Italian city of Pisa.

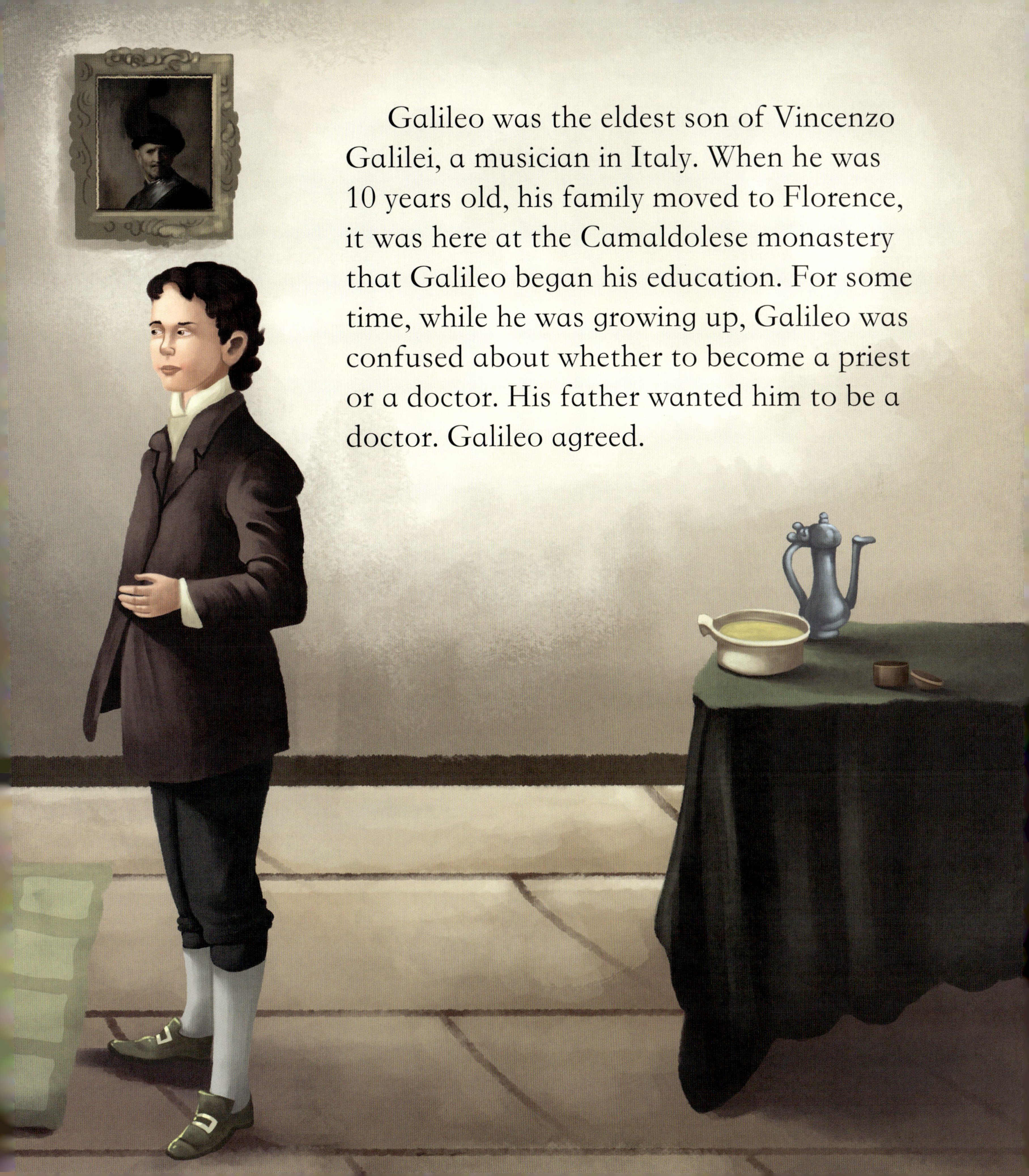

Galileo was the eldest son of Vincenzo Galilei, a musician in Italy. When he was 10 years old, his family moved to Florence, it was here at the Camaldolese monastery that Galileo began his education. For some time, while he was growing up, Galileo was confused about whether to become a priest or a doctor. His father wanted him to be a doctor. Galileo agreed.

Pendulums, levers balls...

In 1581, 17-year-old Galileo went to the University of Pisa to study medicine. But he soon realized he was more interested in maths and physics. So, he stopped studying to become a doctor and began studying science and maths instead. Four years later, Galileo left the university and got a job as a teacher. He began to experiment with pendulums, levers, and balls.

In 1586, Galileo wrote about hydrostatic balance, which is a device to correctly measure weight of things. He also wrote on other topics in science. Because of all his great work, Galileo was becoming famous.

In 1604, Galileo supported an astronomer called Nicolaus Copernicus. Copernicus had said that Sun was the centre of the universe and Earth and other planets revolved around it. At that time, it was believed that Earth was at the centre. The new idea of Earth revolving around the Sun made the Church and religious bodies unhappy.

In 1609, Galileo created a telescope that he is most famous for. He had improved on the design of a telescope made in Holland. With his powerful telescope, Galileo could make objects appear very, very large and could view planets.

Galileo soon started observing the sky with his telescope. He saw the most incredible things. Galileo found that the moon had craters and mountains, while people had thought that the moon was smooth! He found out that the planet Jupiter had moons too. In 1610, Galileo discovered four large moons of Jupiter — Io, Europa, Ganymede, and CallisIo. He also discovered various phases of the planet Venus. Galileo identified spots or patches that appear on the surface of the sun called the sunspots. Galileo's work in astronomy made him really famous.

The Church did not like Galileo supporting Copernicus's theory. He was accused of going against the Bible and was told to stop teaching and spreading the theory. Galileo had to follow the order.

In 1632, Galileo published his book *Dialogue Concerning the Two Chief World Systems.* It was written as a talk between two men discussing Copernicus's theory, with points both for and against the theory. The Church was still very upset and sent Galileo to jail. Later, they allowed him to live at his home under house arrest.

Galileo continued to write while he was under house arrest. In 1638, he became blind. Galileo died on 8 January 1642.

Galileo is known as the 'Father of Modern Science', because of his amazing contribution to the fields of physics, astronomy and mathematics. NASA (National Advisory Committee for Aeronautics) named its spacecraft Galileo in his honour. That spacecraft was sent to study the planet Jupiter and its moons.

The world will always remember Galileo for his incredible work.